Developing literacy Skills

USING POETRY

KEY STAGE 1
P1–3

FRANCES MACKAY

HOPSCOTCH EDUCATIONAL PUBLISHING

✦ Contents ✦

Published by Hopscotch Educational Publishing Company Ltd, Althorpe House, Althorpe Street, Leamington Spa, Warwickshire CV31 2AU.

© 1999 Hopscotch Educational Publishing

Written by Frances Mackay
Foreword by Wes Magee
Series design by Blade Communications
Illustrated by Natalie Inwood
Cover illustration by Susan Hutchison
Printed by Clintplan, Southam

Frances Mackay hereby asserts her moral right to be identified as the author of this work in accordance with the Copyright, Designs and Patents Act, 1988.

ISBN 1-902239-12-1

Introduction

ABOUT THE SERIES

Developing Literacy Skills is a series of books aimed at developing key literacy skills using stories, non-fiction, poetry and rhyme, spelling and grammar, from Key Stage 1 (P1–3) through to Key Stage 2 (P4–7).

The series offers a structured approach which provides detailed lesson plans to teach specific literacy skills. A unique feature of the series is the provision of differentiated photocopiable activities aimed at considerably reducing teacher preparation time. Suggestions for using the photocopiable pages as a stimulus for further work in the classroom are provided to ensure maximum use of this resource.

ABOUT THIS BOOK

This book is for teachers of children at Key Stage 1 and Scottish levels P1–3. It aims to:

◆ develop children's literacy skills through exposure to and experience of a wide range of stimulating poetry with supporting differentiated activities which are both diversified and challenging;

◆ support teachers by providing practical teaching methods based on whole-class, group, paired and individual teaching;

◆ encourage enjoyment and curiosity as well as developing skills of interpretation and response.

CHAPTER CONTENT

◆ Overall aims

These outline the aims for both lessons set out in each chapter.

◆ Featured poems

This lists the poems that are used in the lessons together with the page number on which a photocopiable version of the poem can be found.

◆ Intended learning

This sets out the specific aims for each individual lesson within the chapter.

◆ Starting point

This provides ideas for introducing the activity and may include key questions to ask the children.

◆ Group activities

This explains the task(s) the children will carry out in the lesson without supporting photocopiable activities.

◆ Using the differentiated activity sheets

This explains how to use each sheet as well as providing guidance on the type of child who will benefit most from each sheet.

◆ Plenary session

This suggests ideas for whole-class sessions to discuss the learning outcomes and follow-up work.

◆ Using the photocopiable sheets as a stimulus for further work

This is a useful list of further activities that can be developed from the activity sheets. These ideas maximise the use of the photocopiable pages.

◆ Other ideas for using...

This contains other ideas for developing the skills explored in each chapter. The ideas will have completely different learning intentions from the featured lessons and provide a range of alternatives.

USING THE POETRY PAGES

For shared reading, the poems on these pages could be enlarged by hand or on the photocopier. Alternatively each child or pair could have their own photocopy.

Wes Magee, a well-known poet who provides popular in-school sessions on teaching poetry, explains the level of poetry and related activities that children should be addressing at this age. He also gives several examples of different types of poetry which will prove a useful introduction to a topic sometimes seen as 'difficult to do' with primary school children.

Wordsworth, Shelley, Keats, Milton, Shakespeare… famous names from the world of poetry that induce the feeling of reverence. Names synonymous with poems that appear difficult to the reader. Poems that are larded with classical references and seemingly incomprehensible language.

No wonder most adults shy away from poetry. No wonder it remains a minority interest despite recent publicity attempts to drag it into the modern world such as the establishment of a National Poetry Day, Poems on the Underground, and voting for the Nation's Favourite Poem. Due to its old-fashioned image (all those dead poets) poetry books for adults gather dust on the bookshop shelves.

How different poetry is for children! Publishers fall over themselves in the rush to market poems by **living** authors (Roger McGough, Brian Patten, Judith Nicholls et al) in vibrantly illustrated books. These days one only has to step into a school to be aware of poetry publications in classroom and library: children actually choose to read the stuff!

How, therefore, can we assist children with poetry? What **is** a poem? It helps if we contrast a poem with a story. The first difference is shape.

◆ Shape

Stories are usually printed on the page in solid rectangles except for occasional missing bits where paragraphs appear. **The printer** decides where lines begin and end. Poems, on the other hand, all have different shapes. Lines can be long or short, are often set out in verses, and the **writer** decides where lines begin and end. The shaped (i.e. crafted)

appearance of a verse on the page is a crucial difference between story and poetry. The following verse does not **look** like a story.

> The sky is grey
>
> And flakes are falling.
>
> I hear the snowman
>
> Calling, calling.

◆ Music

Music is another major difference. Poems often (but not always) have rhythm or beat. Stories mostly do not.

Poems are therefore related to other written forms, such as songs or chants. Children will know any number of playground chants passed down orally from generation to generation. Skipping and counting chants such as 'Hey! Bee Sea Dee, Eee Eff Gee!', and 'One potato, two potato, three potato, four', if written down would look like poems. They also have catchily infectious rhythms that make children want to clap hands, sway, or stamp their feet. When it comes to the use of rhythm children can be taught that the poem 'family' is more inclusive than it first appears.

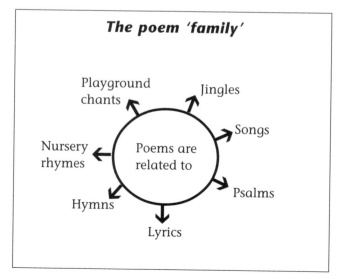

The poem 'family'

Playground chants — Jingles — Songs — Psalms — Lyrics — Hymns — Nursery rhymes → Poems are related to

Many poems have attracted the attention of composers. Children now know Christina Rossetti's 'In the bleak midwinter' and Eleanor Farjeon's 'A morning song' ('Morning has broken…') as songs rather than as poems, which is how they were originally published.

◆ Length

There remains one further major difference between poems and stories where children are concerned: length. Poems, mostly, are short; stories are long. A poem is often contained within a single page; stories occupy many pages. This creates, for children, differences in the reading experience.

The language of poetry is often ultra-precise and condensed: every word counts. Poems require a closer reading, maybe even repeated readings before communication becomes complete. Stories, with their greater length, can afford to be more laid back, discursive and descriptive. The story writer may well take a page to describe a character's appearance (size, hair, clothing, habits) or devote entire paragraphs to events occurring at a family breakfast.

Teachers can help children become acquainted with poems by regularly reading them aloud in class. Children then gain confidence in picking up the poems' story lines (the narratives) and learn to respond to the rhythms. Familiarity, where poems are concerned, breeds understanding and enjoyment.

Thus we have three differences between story and poem: **shape** on the page, the **music/rhythms**, and **length**. If children are aware of such differences they are on the way to learning about and appreciating poetry.

◆ Rhyme

Another aspect of poems now comes into play: rhyme. On my many school visits a question that often crops up is "Does a poem have to rhyme?" Contrary to a popularly held idea (yet another legacy of the dim and distant literary past) poems do not have to rhyme. There are non-rhyming syllable-count poems. There are prose poems. Rhyme is but one of the tools used by a poet when crafting a poem. The writer makes a simple choice: to use rhyme, or not.

However, rhyme is enduringly attractive and popular with children. It begins with nursery rhymes, many of which have a simple a/b/c/b rhyme scheme. 'Incy Wincy Spider' is an example.

Incy Wincy Spider
Climbing up the spout.
Down came the rain
And washed the spider out.

The simple rhyme *spout/out* helps to give the verse a basic rhythm. Such rhymes also help children to speedily memorise the poem. Heard three or four times, the lines stick in the mind… for ever! Such simple poems are the beginning of a child's 'mind reservoir' of literature. Life, even for the very young, is the richer for knowing such pieces. It rather underlines the need for teachers (and parents) to regularly read poems (starting with nursery rhymes) to the very young.

Using Poetry
KS1/P1–3

Developing
Literacy
Skills
5
© Hopscotch Educational Publishing

It is part of the poet's craft to use rhyme inventively. Thus it is not unusual to find countless rhyme variations in books of nursery rhymes or poems for young children. 'Pat-a-Cake' uses an a/a/b/b rhyme pattern:

> Pat-a-cake, pat-a-cake, baker's man
> bake me a cake as fast as you can.
> Pat it and prick it, and mark it with T,
> Put it in the oven for Tommy and me.

Rhyme as employed in 'Charlie Warlie' gives an altogether different verbal and rhythmic effect:

> Charlie Warlie had a cow,
> Black and white upon her brow
> Open the gate and let her through
> Charlie Warlie's old cow.

There we have a single rhyme chime *cow/brow/cow*, a half rhyme (*brow/through*), and an internal rhyme (*Charlie Warlie*). What seems at first sight an incredibly simple nursery verse in fact uses a number of rhyme skills.

Language

One doesn't want to destroy the enjoyment of po}try for children by dissecting every last stanza (another word for verse) for use of technique but knowledge of how a poem is constructed does help teachers' confidence when they are dealing with such literary objects. The mystique of poetry is to an extent removed, and poems can be seen for what they are – items of language communication.

Once nursery rhymes become inappropriate (around the age of five), more complex poems come

into play. Imagery and 'colour' in language is evident, as in this list poem, 'What is the Sun?'

> The Sun is an orange dinghy
>   sailing across a calm sea.
> It is a gold coin
>   dropped down a drain in heaven.
> The Sun is a red thumb-print
>   on a sheet of pale blue paper.
> It is a milk bottle's gold top
>   floating in a puddle.

Note the visual shape on the page. There is no rhyme, but there is imagery (or metaphor). The first of each two lines is a simple image; the second of each two lines two extends the image.

The use of rhyme, too, becomes more inventive and interesting, as in this clapping song (poem)…

> Our school band
> our school band
> best band heard
> in all the land
> start at teacher's
> sharp command
>   in
>   our
>   school
>   band.

A single rhyme (*band/land/command/band*), an absence of punctuation (to help create a slightly breathless effect), a rhythm that changes as the shape of the verse alters towards the end, and a crying need for the piece to be chanted out loud. Just one example of how poems for children can carry great variety and aural impact.

Foreword

Young children enjoy the way in which poets play with words. There's a delicious feeling of experimentation in such lines as…

> Ploffskin, Pluffskin, Pelican jee!
> We think no birds so happy as we!

and…

> Puddle and Peel
> packed their
> pink pants
> in panniers
> and pedalled away
> to Paris.

Wes Magee is a former primary school teacher and headteacher. He has been a full-time author since 1989. For information on his services for schools, telephone 01751 417633.

Acknowledgements

The author and publisher gratefully acknowledge permission to reproduce copyright material in this book.

'Hats' by Daphne Lister. Reprinted by permission of the author.

'Pick'n' Mix Zoo' © 1995, John Foster from *Action Rhymes* compiled by John Foster (Oxford University Press), included by permission of the author.

'Exercises' (p19, 9 lines) from *One Blue Boat* by Linda Hammond (Viking, 1991) copyright © Linda Hammond, 1991. Reproduced by permission of the author.

'The Bird' by Tony Mitton. Reprinted with the permission of the author.

'Squeezes' (p11, 4 lines) from *Gargling with Jelly* by Brian Patten (Viking, 1985) copyright © Brian Patten, 1985. Reproduced by permission of Penguin Books Ltd.

'Granny Granny Please Comb My Hair' by Grace Nichols. Reprinted with permission of Curtis Brown Ltd, London, on behalf of Grace Nichols. Copyright © Grace Nichols, 1984.

'Down by the School Gate' by Wes Magee. Reprinted by permission of the author.

'Wet Playtime' by David Ward. Reprinted by permission of the author.

'School is Great' (p80, 14 lines) from *Please Mrs Butler* by Allan Ahlberg (Kestrel, 1983) copyright © Allan ahlberg, 1983. Reprinted by permission of Penguin Books Ltd.

'A Swamp Romp' by Doug MacLeod. Reprinted by permission of the author.

Every effort has been made to trace the owners of copyright of poems in this book and the publisher apologises for any inadvertant omissions. Any persons claiming copyright for any material should contact the publisher who will be happy to pay the permissions fees requested and who will amend the information in this book on any subsequent reprint.

Overall aims

- To understand and use correctly terms about rhymes, such as: letter, word, line, beginning, end, rhyme, title.
- To understand that a line of writing is not necessarily a sentence.
- To re-read a variety of familiar rhymes.
- To understand and be able to create rhyme through recognising, exploring and working with rhyming patterns.
- To use knowledge of rhyme to identify families of rhyming words.

 ## Featured poems (page 56)

A selection of rhymes

 ## LESSON ONE

 ## Intended learning

- To understand and use correctly terms about rhymes, such as: letter, word, line, beginning, end, rhyme, title.
- To understand that a line of writing is not necessarily a sentence.
- To re-read a familiar rhyme.

Starting point: Whole class

- Make a large copy of 'Humpty Dumpty' on a piece of paper or the board. Include the title.
- Ask the children how many of them know the rhyme already. Show them the rhyme. Tell them that the name of a rhyme can also be called the title, so the title of this rhyme is 'Humpty Dumpty' (point to the words as you say them). Ask some children to come out and point to the title – repeat it together.
- Read out the rhyme, pointing to each word as you say it. Ask the children what the rhyme means.
- Explain that the rhyme has four lines in it and point to each one. Tell them that the first line has

six words in it. Ask someone to count and point to each word. Count and point to each word in the next three lines.

- Ask the children to point to the capital letters in the rhyme. Explain that capitals are always used for names. Who in the class has a name beginning with these letters? When else do we use capital letters? Explain that rhymes and poems nearly always have capital letters at the beginning of each line and that they differ from stories in this way. Look at other rhymes in a book or on page 56 to show this.
- Remind the children how we end sentences with full stops. Ask them to show you the full stops in the rhyme. Discuss the fact that the full stops come at the end of the sentence, not at the end of the line.

Group activities

- Make a game out of finding words, full stops or capital letters. Provide the children with copies of the rhyme explored in the lesson and challenge them to colour the capital letters, full stops or particular words. Who can find them all? More able children could colour each sentence a different colour (to differentiate between sentences and lines).
- With adult support, some children could act out each line of the rhyme while others say the words.
- Write the words of the rhyme on pieces of card. Ask the children to sort the words into the poem using an enlarged version as a model.

Plenary session

Bring the whole class together again to share the group activities. Revise the terms such as 'title', 'word', 'capital letter', 'line' and 'sentence' by using the children's work as examples. Watch some of the children act out the rhyme. Ask the class to check if the children doing the last activity have set out their poem correctly – is there the correct number of lines? Are the words in the right places?

◆LESSON TWO◆

◆ Intended learning

◆ To understand and be able to create rhyme through recognising, exploring and working with rhyming patterns.
◆ To use knowledge of rhyme to identify families of rhyming words.
◆ To re-read a variety of familiar rhymes.

◆ Starting point: Whole class

◆ Using the enlarged version of 'Humpty Dumpty' again, remind the children of the activities in Lesson One. Can they tell you where the capital letters/full stops/lines/sentences are?
◆ Ask them to look at the end of the first two lines. What do they notice? Explain the term 'rhyme' and ask them to tell you any other words they know that rhyme with *wall* and *fall*. Write these on the board and add some more of your own to the list. (ball, call, hall, small, tall, football). If appropriate, discuss how the word endings can be different but still make the same sound (as in lines three and four of the rhyme).
◆ Make an enlarged version of 'Hickety Pickety, My Black Hen'. Ask the children to find the words that rhyme as you read the lines. Make up word families by selecting certain words from the rhyme, such as *hen*. Point out that the onset has changed but the rime has remained the same.

> h<u>en</u>
> p<u>en</u>
> m<u>en</u>

Use magnetic letters to do this.
◆ Write a list of words on the board using a rime from one of the two rhymes, such as *wall, call, tall, ball, hall* and *day, lay, say, today, bay, play*. Can the children sort the words into two rhyming families?
◆ Tell the children they will now have an opportunity to find out more about rhymes themselves.

◆ Using the differentiated activity sheets

Activity sheet 1

This activity is for children who need further experience in hearing and identifying rhyming words. An adult will need to share the poem with the children.

Activity sheet 2

This activity is for children who can identify rhyming words and can record this by analogy.

Activity sheet 3

This activity is for children who can recognise sounds from the alphabet and join them to a rhyme to generate words. An adult should share the full versions of the poems on page 56 with the children before they begin the task.

◆ Plenary session

Bring the whole class together again when the children have completed their tasks. Share some of the children's work from each group. Can others think of more rhyming words for each activity? Write up a whole-class list. Tell the children that exploring rhyming families like these helps us to spell words, for if we know how to spell 'cat', we can easily spell 'bat', just by changing the beginning letter. Explore this further.

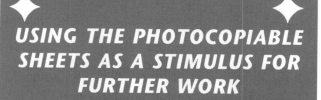

USING THE PHOTOCOPIABLE SHEETS AS A STIMULUS FOR FURTHER WORK

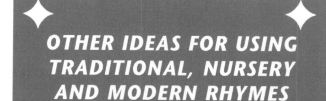

OTHER IDEAS FOR USING TRADITIONAL, NURSERY AND MODERN RHYMES

✦ Make a class rhyming picture dictionary, beginning with the words on the activity sheets. Encourage the children to refer to the dictionary for their writing.

✦ Play Onset and Rime Snap. Give the children two piles of cards, one with a variety of onsets and the other with rimes. They turn over a card from each pile and if a word is made, they call out the word.

✦ Encourage the children to make up their own endings for the rhymes:
> To market, to market,
> To buy a fat sheep,
> Home again, home again,
> Jiggety-weep.

✦ Play Hunt the Rhyme. Select one of the words from an activity sheet. Challenge the children to find other words that rhyme with it in selected texts, such as story books, picture dictionaries, poetry books and so on.

✦ Make a display of pictures and objects with a common rhyme. Encourage the children to add their own things to the display.

✦ Challenge the children using Activity sheet 3 to make their own word family wheels using rimes from their own spellings lists or reading.

✦ Play Rhyming Snap by asking the children to match cards with pictures of things that rhyme.

✦ Make a class book of traditional rhymes by asking the children to select their favourites from a collection. Share the book with a local playgroup or nursery.

✦ Reinforce the rhymes through rhythm with lots of aural re-reading and learning of highly patterned rhymes. Clap or play musical instruments to support the children.

✦ Ask the children to illustrate the rhymes and then to label them using words from the poems to aid development of comprehension and word recognition.

✦ Encourage the children to make up actions to go with the rhymes to help them learn the words.

✦ Invite the children to bring in their own collections of rhymes from home. Encourage them to share their favourite ones with others and say why they like them. Invite parents in to share their favourites with the class.

✦ Explore alliterations in traditional rhymes. Encourage the children to write their own alliterations.

✦ Ask older children to act out well-known rhymes. Can the children guess which one it is?

◆ Rhyming words ◆

✦ Look at the pictures. Say the words out loud. Draw a line
  from the pictures that rhyme with 'bat' to the poem. One
  has been done for you.

Bat, bat,
Come under my hat,
And I'll give you a slice of bacon;
And when I bake,
I'll give you a cake,
If I'm not mistaken.

✦ On the back of this page draw pictures of other words that rhyme
  with 'bat', such as 'rat' and 'sunhat'.

Developing
Literacy
Skills

◆ Rhyming words ◆

◆ Look at the pictures to go with this rhyme. Then look at the other pictures. Write the rhyming words underneath.

Hickety, pickety, my black hen,
She lays eggs for gentlemen;

m _____

p _____

t _____

Gentlemen come every day
To see what my black hen doth lay.

lay

h _____

M _____

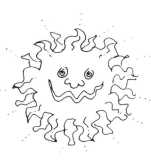

r _____

pl _____   spr _____

Developing
Literacy
Skills

Photocopiable

✦ Rhyming words ✦

✦ Read the rhymes. Make word families by writing words in
the boxes. The first ones have been done for you.

Sing, sing,
What shall I sing?
The cat's run away
With the pudding string!

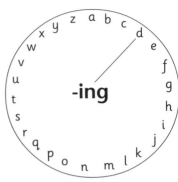

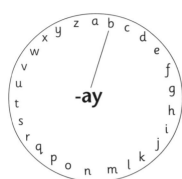

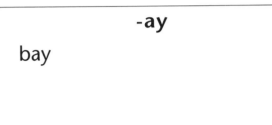

-ing	**-ay**
ding	bay

To market, to market,
To buy a fat pig,
Home again, home again,
Jiggety-jig.

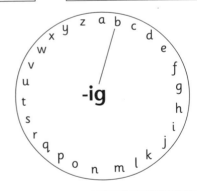

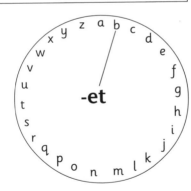

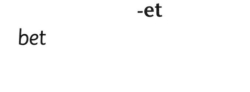

-ig	**-et**
big	bet

Developing
Literacy
Skills   Photocopiable
© Hopscotch Educational Publishing   13

Overall aims

+ To re-read and recite poems with predictable and repeating patterns.
+ To extend and invent patterns.
+ To use predictable patterns as models for own writing.
+ To identify and explore alliteration.
+ To investigate plurals.

 ## *Featured poems (page 57)*

As Wet as a Fish and **One Orange Owlet** – both anonymous
Hats by Daphne Lister
Pick 'N' Mix Zoo by Celia Warren
Walking Round the Zoo by John Foster

 ## LESSON ONE

 ## *Intended learning*

+ To re-read and recite poems with predictable and repeating patterns.
+ To extend and invent patterns.
+ To use predictable patterns as models for own writing.

 ## *Starting point: Whole class*

+ Enlarge a copy of the poem 'Walking Round the Zoo'. Have ready some pictures of the animals mentioned in the poem.
+ Read the poem to the class, making sure the children can see the words as you say them. Ask them to tell you what the person in the poem saw when walking round the zoo. Show the pictures of each animal. Ask the children if they have been to a zoo. What animals have they seen there? Re-read the poem together.
+ Point out that the poem begins with a question – read it out. What do they notice about the other three verses? Talk about how the poem uses the same lines to open each verse – it repeats itself. What else do they notice about the words used? Discuss the rhyming pattern.
+ Tell the children that they are going to make up their own poem about walking round the zoo. Ask them to work with a partner for a few minutes to think of a sentence about an animal they might see at the zoo. Share their ideas and write out a class poem using the same pattern as the original poem. Recite the new poem together. Consider performance skills, such as the use of volume and emphasis on particular words.

 ## *Group activities*

+ Provide one group with the words:
  Walking round the zoo,
  What did I see?
on card. Ask them to complete the verse by adding a sentence as in the whole-class session. The number of verses to complete could depend on the children's ability levels.
+ Another group could work together to recite and invent actions for the original poem.
+ More able children could use the same repeating patterns and structure of the original poem, but write their own poem. For example, 'Walking Round the School' or 'Walking round the Park'.

Plenary session

Bring the whole class together again when the children have completed their tasks. Share the poems invented by the children. Discuss any problems they may have had and how they solved them. Ask some children to read or say their poem out loud. The other children could be encouraged to add actions to the poem. Watch the performance of Group 2. Discuss ways in which the performance could be improved.

◆ LESSON TWO ◆

◆ Intended learning

- ◆ To use predictable patterns as models for own writing.
- ◆ To identify and explore alliteration.
- ◆ To investigate plurals.

◆ Starting point: Whole class

- ◆ Enlarge a copy of the poem 'One Orange Owlet' and read it out, making sure the children can see the poem as you read it. Discuss the contents to make sure the children understand the meaning of the words. Re-read the poem together.
- ◆ What do they notice about the poem? Is there a pattern? Discuss how each line counts upwards in numbers and how each word in each line begins with the same letter. Tell them the special name for this (alliteration). Explore alliterations by making up simple ones using the children's names. For example, 'Peter picked up a pineapple' and 'Mary made marmalade'.
- ◆ Next, refer back to the poem and challenge the children to think up other alliterations that could fit the poem, such as 'one old orang-utan', 'two tiny trees', 'three thorny thistles' and 'four fine fellows'. Show them how using a dictionary can help them find suitable words. Write them on the board.
- ◆ Ask the children to tell you what they notice about the end words of each line in the poem. Using the poem, explain how to make words plural by adding 's'. For example, if there were more than one owlet, how would it be spelled? If there was only one trumpet, how would it be spelled? Tell the children that they might need to remember this when they complete their next activity.

◆ Using the differentiated activity sheets

Activity sheet 1

This activity provides picture-clue support for younger or less able readers. It involves sequencing the poem in correct counting order.

Activity sheet 2

This activity provides children with words to copy to complete the poem but it also encourages them to explore their own ideas.

Activity sheet 3

This activity is for more independent workers. It encourages them to use a dictionary to write the poem within a set framework.

◆ Plenary session

Bring the whole class together again to share poems from each group. How many different alliterations could be found for the same numbers? Make up whole-class alliterations using all the children's ideas. How long a sentence can they make? Check that the children have added 's' for plurals. If appropriate, explain that some words have different endings for plurals.

Developing Literacy Skills

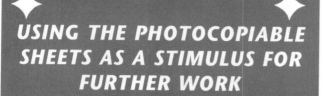

USING THE PHOTOCOPIABLE SHEETS AS A STIMULUS FOR FURTHER WORK

✦ Challenge the children to make actions to go with their poems. Encourage them to recite the poem until they are ready to perform it to others.

✦ Make the poems into counting books. Ask the children to illustrate each page.

✦ Make up a class dictionary, starting with the words on Activity sheet 2. Make up alliterative sentences using the dictionary.

✦ Encourage the children to find other poems with alliterations in them. Share them with the class. Make a display of the poems.

✦ Play alliteration games – 'I went to the shops and I bought a book, a bed, a basin' and so on.

✦ Make mobiles of the words in the poems, in singular and plural, for the children to use as a resource bank of words.

✦ Dramatise the poems.

✦ Display the poems as a counting frieze in the maths area of the classroom.

✦ Make up word searches of words beginning with the same letter.

✦ Make two copies of Activity sheet 1, cut them out and glue onto card. The children could play Snap to help develop their sight vocabulary.

✦ Make word trees with the selected letter written in the trunk and alliterative sentences in the branches.

OTHER IDEAS FOR USING POEMS WITH PREDICTABLE PATTERNS

✦ Add further verses to poems by copying the pattern. Carry out as a whole-class activity first and then encourage group efforts.

✦ Alter existing poems by using the same lines but substituting new words, for example, using 'Pick 'N' Mix Zoo' (page 57):
Marshmallow mallards,
Cheetah drops
Red jelly eagles,
Llama lollipops

✦ Develop rhyming patterns further by adding more words, for example, using 'Hats' on page 57:
A hat for a hamster,
*A hat for a **dog**,*
A hat for a goldfish,
*A hat for a **frog**,*
A hat for a guinea-pig,
*A hat for a **hog***
and so on where every second line rhymes.

✦ **Other ideas for using the poems on page 57**
– Use 'As Wet as a Fish' to introduce work on antonyms.
– Link 'Walking Round the Zoo' with 'Hats' by sharing the funny idea of animals wearing hats. Challenge the children to think of zoo animals that could be written into the poem 'Hats'. Retain the last four lines of the original poem and ask the children to count how many hats there would be in their new poem.
– 'Pick 'N' Mix Zoo' is a good poem to use to investigate syllables. It will go well with musical accompaniments as it has a definite rhythm. The children could also find the alliterations in the poem and make up alternative lines so the whole poem has alliterations, such as 'crocodile chocs' or 'toffee tigers'.

◆ A counting poem ◆

◆ Colour in the pictures. Cut out the boxes. Put them in the right order to make a counting poem. Glue them onto another piece of paper.

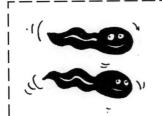 two

thin things

five

fine frogs

 one

fit fleas

 four

tiny tadpoles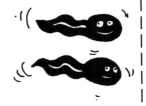

 three

old owl

♦ A counting poem ♦

♦ Finish this counting poem by choosing words from each box or adding your own. Make sure the words in each line begin with the same letter. You may need to add an 's' to some words.

One _____

Two _____

Three _____

Four _____

Five _____

Six _____

Seven _____

Are coming to get you!

old	orange
tiny	tame
thin	thick
fat	fast
small	sad

owl	octopus
tiger	tadpole
thing	thumb
fish	finger
spider	snail

Developing
Literacy
Skills

◆ A counting poem ◆

◆ Finish this counting poem. Make sure the words in each line begin with the same letter.

Use a dictionary to help you.

One _____ octopus

Two terrible _____

Three thorny things

Four _____ frogs

Five funny _____

Six _____ snakes

Seven silly _____

Eight enormous _____

Nine nice _____

Ten _____ tigers

Are coming to get you!

◆ Draw a picture of one of the creatures from your poem.

Overall aims

- To learn and recite simple poems with actions.
- To explore action poems by introducing new words and lines.
- To use action poems as models for own writing.

 ## Featured poems (page 58)

We Can Play the Big Bass Drum – anonymous
Exercises by Linda Hammond
The Bird by Tony Mitton

 ## LESSON ONE

 ## Intended learning

- To learn and recite simple poems with actions.
- To explore action poems by introducing new words and lines.

 ## Starting point: Whole class

- Choose either 'Exercises' or 'We Can Play the Big Bass Drum'. Tell the children that they are going to learn a poem with actions to it.
  'Exercises' – share an enlarged version of the poem with the children. Recite the poem together, then ask the children to suggest some actions to go with each line. Agree the actions and recite the lines one at a time. Then put the whole poem together with all the actions.
  'We Can Play the Big Bass Drum' – tell the children that some poems can use lots of different actions like the one they are now going to share. Explain that it is about musical instruments. Share an enlarged version of the first verse. Teach the children the words. Agree on a suitable action for 'And this is the way to do it'. Act out the verse several times. Divide the class into three groups and teach each group to say the words for the sound of the drum, horn and double bass. Show

them pictures of the musical instruments and ask them to work out suitable actions for each one. Then put the whole poem together with the whole class saying the first two lines together, each group saying their own line for the sound of their instrument and the whole class saying 'And this is the way to do it' with the accompanying actions. Go through several times until the children can recite the poem accurately.

 ## Group activities

- The children could work in groups to add another verse to 'We Can Play the Big Bass Drum' poem by adding more instruments and accompanying actions. Tell them that each group will perform the poem to the others at the end of the session.
- The children could learn 'Exercises' as a group and agree the actions. They could introduce some new words to change the actions in the poem, for example:
  Bend your body,
  touch your feet.
  Straighten up
  and touch your ears.

 ## Plenary session

Bring the whole class together again to share the performances. Then allow time for the whole class to join in with the poem as it is recited again. Tell the children what was particularly good about their performances. Discuss how accurate we may need to be when miming some of the actions – can they be improved in any way? Talk about the types of instruments added to the music poem – show pictures of them if possible.

◆ LESSON TWO ◆

◆ Intended learning

◆ To explore action poems by introducing new words and lines.
◆ To use action poems as models for own writing.

◆ Starting point: Whole class

◆ Before the lesson, enlarge the poem 'The Bird'. Draw some separate pictures of a bird's legs, beak, wings and a whole bird on cards.
◆ Remind the children about the action poem(s) shared in Lesson One. Tell them that they will be sharing another action poem today and then writing their own.
◆ Read 'The Bird' to the class, making sure the children can see the words. Show a picture of the bird's legs. Ask the children what actions they could do to show how the legs might walk along. Do the same for the other pictures to go with the bird poem. Agree on the actions for each verse.
◆ Nominate a child to hold up each picture as the poem is re-read. The other children do the actions that go with it. Recite the whole poem together.
◆ Discuss the rhyming pattern in the poem. Can the children suggest alternative words that rhyme and still fit the poem?
◆ Explain that we can use this poem as a model to write a new one. Keep the first line of each verse and together think up alternative endings. For example:

Here are the legs
that wiggle and squirm.
Here is the beak
that catches the worm.
Here are the wings
that make the bird fly
And here is the bird
up in the sky.

Use the same actions to accompany the poem.
◆ Tell the children they will now have the opportunity to write their own action poem in a similar way.

◆ Using the differentiated activity sheets

Activity sheet 1

This activity provides a lot of support and enables children to use a set framework to 'write' a poem.

Activity sheet 2

This activity enables children to select words from a given choice to complete a poem.

Activity sheet 3

This activity is for more independent workers. It requires them to select words from a word box or use a dictionary to complete a poem and then asks them to write one of their own.

◆ Plenary session

Bring the whole class together again when the children have completed their poems. Ask someone from each group to say or read their poem. How many different words can be used so the poems still make sense? Compare the actions for each poem. Which ones do the children like best/think are more appropriate? What problems did they have completing the tasks? How did they solve them?

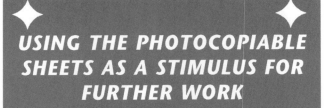

USING THE PHOTOCOPIABLE SHEETS AS A STIMULUS FOR FURTHER WORK

✦ The children using Activity sheet 3 could use the poem as a model to write a different poem about another animal. For example:

> **The Cat**
> *Here are the eyes*
> *that peep and stare.*
> *Here are the claws*
> *that scratch my chair.*
> *Here are the teeth*
> *that bite and snap.*
> *And here is the cat*
> *curled in my lap.*

✦ The children could look for other poems about animals and make up actions to go with them. Put them all into a book and add the anthology to the class library.

✦ The poems and accompanying actions could form the basis for drama work about animals. The children could mime animal actions for others to guess the creature or make up short plays about animals.

✦ Turn the poems into a short play involving a dog, rabbit, bird and mouse. Introduce each character in the play by reading out the relevant poem.

✦ Ask the children to draw the animals in the poems and label the body parts. Compare the animals with humans.

✦ Invite the children to write a story using the animal on their activity sheet as the main character.

✦ Ask the children to find out about caring for different pets. They could start with the ones on the activity sheets.

OTHER IDEAS FOR USING ACTION POEMS

✦ Use action poems as warm-up and cool down activities in PE lessons.

✦ Make up group or whole-class action poems about life in school by listing all the actions the children do before school, during lessons, at play and so on. Use the structure of a poem the children know already and change the words and lines to suit.

✦ Use action poems as a starting point for work on verbs. Make up action word books with drawings and words to describe the action. Older or more able children could also use a thesaurus to find synonyms for the verbs.

✦ Challenge the children to make musical accompaniments to action poems.

✦ Use action poems as a starting point for writing simple instructions or lists. For example, the children could list the different musical instruments in 'We Can Play the Big Bass Drum' and add other instruments to the list. This could be illustrated and displayed.

✦ The children could invent symbols or signs for each action in a poem. These could be written on cards and one child elected to lead the class in a performance of the poem, holding up the cards as appropriate.

✦ Animal actions ✦

✦ Cut out the pictures and put them in the correct place so the poem makes sense.

Dog

Here is the [   ] that wags,

Here are the [   ] so big,

Here is the [   ] that sniffs,

And here are the [   ] that dig.

paws

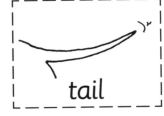
ears

tail

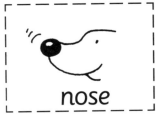
nose

✦ Now make up some actions to go with the poem.

23

✦ Animal actions ✦

✦ Put the correct words in the spaces to finish this action poem.

The Rabbit

Here are the _____ (nose, ears)
so furry and big.

Here are the _____ (claws, teeth)
that love to dig.

Here is the _____ (eyes, tail)
so soft and round.

And here are the _____ (feet, legs)
that thump the ground.

✦ Draw a picture of the rabbit and label the parts of its body.

✦ Now make up some actions to go with the poem.

Photocopiable
© Hopscotch Educational Publishing

◆ Animal actions ◆

◆ Read this poem about a bird.

The Bird
Here are the legs
that walk along.

Here is the beak
that sings a song.

Here are the wings
that flap and spread.

And here is the bird
above my head.

Tony Mitton

◆ Now choose words from the box below or use a dictionary
to finish this poem about a mouse. Make up some actions
to go with the poem.

The Mouse
Here are the ears
so _____ and round.

Here are the legs
that _____ around.

Here is the tail
that swishes and _____ .

And here is the nose
that _____ all day.

small	big
little	furry
walk	run
scamper	scuttle
flicks	sways
moves	jumps
sniffs	twitches
smells	moves

◆ Now make up an action poem of your own.

Overall aims

- To read a variety of poems about family life.
- To relate poems to own experience.
- To use poems as a stimulus for own writing.
- To make collections of words related to families.

Featured poems (page 59)

Squeezes by Brian Patten
Granny Granny Please Comb My Hair
by Grace Nichols
My Dad by Frances Mackay

LESSON ONE

Intended learning

- To read a variety of poems about family life.
- To relate poems to own experience.
- To use poems as a stimulus for own writing.

Starting point: Whole class

- Talk about the many different kinds of families and how one family can be very different from another. (You may need to treat this subject with sensitivity. Be aware of the children's backgrounds.)
- Ask the children to tell you some of the things they like to do with people in their families. Make a list on the board. Tell them about something you enjoy doing with your family.
- Ask them to tell you what they do if someone in their family is feeling sad. Then read the poem 'Squeezes' by Brian Patten to give an example of one way of doing this!
- Ask the children what they like best about older members of their family, such as grandparents. Tell them that the girl in the next poem they are going to share likes her grandmother because she has lots of time to spend with her and is not as busy as her mother. Now share 'Granny Granny

Please Comb My Hair' by Grace Nichols. Talk about what is happening in the poem. What kind of things do the children enjoy when they are with their grandparents or older family members?

Group activities

- One group could list the things they enjoy doing with their parents, siblings or grandparents and then turn to a friend or an adult in the group and tell them about some of these things.
- Another group could build up a word bank of family words by drawing three circles (or just one if appropriate) with the name of a family member inside the circle and then words around it to describe the things they do together. For example:

The children could then use these words to write some sentences about the things they enjoy doing with this person.
- More able children could be encouraged to write about a particular incident/outing/event they remember doing with a family member and why that time was so important to them.

Plenary session

Bring the whole class together again when the children have completed the tasks. Ask someone from each group to share their discussions and/or writing. From the discussion, add to the list of things families enjoy doing together. Discuss why the children think these times are best.

◆ LESSON TWO ◆

◆ Intended learning

- ◆ To use a poem as a stimulus for building up a collection of words about families.
- ◆ To write a description of a family member.

◆ Starting point: Whole class

- ◆ Remind the children about the activities carried out in Lesson One. Tell them that they will be doing some more work about families today.
- ◆ Ask them to remind you of the names of some of the people who can belong to a family, such as 'Mum', 'Dad', 'step-mother', 'step-father', 'brother' and 'foster sister'. Write them on the board.
- ◆ Circle the word 'Dad' and tell the children that you are going to read them a poem about somebody's father. Read out an enlarged version of 'My Dad', making sure the children can see the words. Ask them to tell you what this person thinks of their dad. What kind of person is he? What does he look like?
- ◆ Have ready a drawing of the dad described in the poem. Read out each line again, one at a time, and use words from the poem to label the drawing, such as 'black beard', 'no hair' and 'bushy eyebrows'. What other words can the children think of to describe him? Add these words to the drawing.
- ◆ Ask the children to think up sentences to describe the dad in the poem using some of these labels. Talk about the correct use of capital letters and full stops. Write the sentences on the board.
- ◆ Ask the children to think about one person in their family, then to spend a few minutes telling a friend about this person – what they look like, what they wear and so on.
- ◆ Tell the children that they will now have an opportunity to draw and write about this person in more detail.

◆ Using the differentiated activity sheets

Activity sheet 1

This activity requires the children to respond to the poems they have been hearing and talking about by drawing a picture of a family member and writing some words and a sentence about him or her.

Activity sheet 2

This activity requires the children to select words to describe a family member and then use three of these words to write some sentences.

Activity sheet 3

This activity requires the children to use selected words to write six sentences about a chosen family member.

◆ Plenary session

Bring the whole class together again when the children have completed their descriptions. Ask some children from each group to show their pictures and read their sentences. Use the time to check that capital letters and full stops have been used correctly by praising children who have succeeded at doing this. Compare the words selected by the children in group 2 to describe their person. What words would the children use to describe themselves? Make a list of these words to use as a resource bank for further writing.

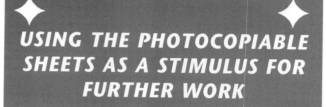

Family poems

USING THE PHOTOCOPIABLE SHEETS AS A STIMULUS FOR FURTHER WORK

✦ Make books about the children's families, starting with the work on the activity sheets. Encourage the children to bring in photographs that can be added to the books. Ask them to find or write simple poems that describe their family members.

✦ Build on the describing words by asking the children to complete a simple profile of themselves, such as hair and eye colour, favourite game, where they live, pets and so on. Use the profile to make a class 'passport'. Family passports could also be made.

✦ Ask the children to write a letter to the person they have drawn (if it is a very young child, write to the parent) and ask the person to write back to them at school. Share the letters.

✦ Ask the children to draw their own family tree with the names of people in the trunk and sentences about the family members on the branches, beginning with those sentences they have written on the activity sheets.

✦ Explore word endings and beginnings using family words, for example: -er words (brother, sister, mother, father) or -y words (family, happy, friendly, naughty).

✦ Ask the children to fold a large sheet of paper in half and draw their house on the outside cover. Inside, they can draw family members and write sentences about them.

✦ Ask the children to complete sentences about family members, such as: 'My gran is special because…', 'My Dad is funny because…'. Find poems to match, such as: 'Daddy Fell into the Pond' by Alfred Noyes.

OTHER IDEAS FOR USING FAMILY POEMS

✦ Build up a collection of family poems. Challenge the children to select poems for specific reasons, such as poems that 'describe my dad in a bad mood', poems that tell you 'how annoying my sister can be', poems that say 'how much I love my mum' and so on.

✦ Read and share poems about families in other places/cultures. Discuss how similar/different family life can be.

✦ Build up a chronological time-line mural of poems by finding poems about babies, toddlers, young children, teenagers, parents and older people. Ask the children to draw pictures and write sentences to match the poems. Use the display as a discussion starter for subjects such as growing up and the human life cycle.

✦ Challenge the children to write poems about particular families in story books, such as the *Happy Families* series by Allan Ahlberg.

✦ Use family poems as discussion starters to talk about problems/issues that affect the children, such as feelings about a new baby, rivalry between siblings, being a foster child, having only one parent and so on. A suitable collection would be *All in the Family* compiled by John Foster (Oxford University Press).

✦ Make a large display of a family with body outlines of people. Invite the children to select their favourite poems to fill the bodies, such as poems about babies, about mothers and so on.

✦ My family ✦

✦ Draw a picture of someone in your family.

✦ In the box below, write some words about this person.

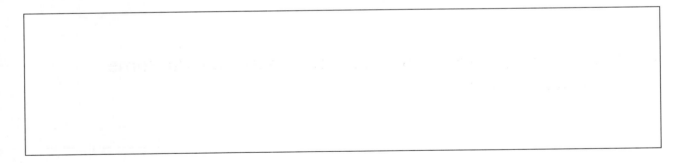

✦ Use some of these words to write a sentence.

_____

◆ My family ◆

◆ Draw a picture of someone in your family. Circle some words to describe this person.

young   good

old   naughty

tall   funny

small   brave

happy   loud

kind   quiet

sad   friendly

helpful   busy

◆ Now use three of the words you have circled to write some sentences about this person.

_____

_____

_____

Developing literacy Skills

◆ My family ◆

◆ Draw the face of someone in your family. Write his or her name.

This person is my

_____.

This person is called

_____.

◆ Now write a description of this person by using each of these words in a sentence. Use a dictionary to help you.

hair   _____

eyes   _____

face   _____

clothes _____

enjoys _____

house _____

Overall aims

- To read poems about school.
- To relate poems to own experience.
- To use poems as a stimulus for own writing.
- To re-read poems taking into account the use of punctuation.
- To identify and discuss patterns of rhythm and rhyme and other features of sound.
- To discriminate syllables in multi-syllabic words.

Featured poems (page 60)

School is Great by Allan Ahlberg
Wet Playtime by Dave Ward
Down by the School Gate by Wes Magee

Intended learning

- To relate a poem to own experience.
- To re-read a poem taking into account the use of punctuation.
- To use a poem as a stimulus for own writing.

Starting point: Whole class

- Ask the children what they like best about school. List of some of their ideas on the board. Choose some of the things mentioned in the poem 'School is Great' by Allan Ahlberg and tell them that you are going to read them a poem about someone who also enjoys these things.
- Read an enlarged version of the poem with the children, making sure they can see the words. Ask them to tell you what things the person in the poem enjoys about school. Add these to the class list.
- Point out that there are also some things in the poem the person does not like. Re-read the poem and ask the children to listen carefully to tell you what these things are. Make three columns on the board and write the headings: 'Do not like', 'Like'

and 'Like very much'. Sort the things in the poem under the correct headings.

- Point out the use of an exclamation mark at the end of some lines to emphasise the things the person likes best. Practise reading these lines together to accentuate the exclamation mark.
- Ask the children to tell you how they think the other lines in the poem should be read. Discuss the use of the comma for pauses and full stops to mark the end of each verse. Reread the poem taking into account the use of punctuation.
- Tell the children they will now have the opportunity to think and write about their own likes and dislikes at school.

Group activities

- Working in pairs or small groups, the children could divide a page into three columns with the headings 'Do not like', 'Like' and 'Like very much' then draw or write a list of things in each column. More able children or those with adult support could then use these words to write a simple school poem of their own, using a repeating pattern for each verse, for example:

   School
   Writing is good,
   But PE is better!
   Singing is good,
   But cooking is better!

 Plenary session

Bring the whole class together again when the children have completed their lists and poems. Ask some of them to share their lists. Do others agree with them? What is the least favourite thing enjoyed at school? What is the most favourite? Share some of the poems. Recite one of them together, making sure the children take notice of the punctuation. Have fun by over-emphasising the exclamation marks.

32
© Hopscotch Educational Publishing

Developing
literacy
Skills

Using poetry
KS1/P1-3

◆ LESSON TWO ◆

◆ Intended learning

◆ To identify and discuss patterns of rhythm and rhyme and other features of sound.
◆ To discriminate syllables in multi-syllabic words.

◆ Starting point: Whole class

◆ Remind the children about the poem read in Lesson One. Tell them that they will now be sharing another one. Read an enlarged version of 'Wet Playtime' by Dave Ward with them, making sure they can see the words. Discuss the meaning of the poem. Are wet playtimes like this at school?

◆ Ask them to tell you anything they notice about the words in the poem. Discuss the repeating sound of -atter words such as: *chatter, matter, batter, clatter, fatter, splatter* and so on. Why do they think the poet has used these words? Compare them to the sound of rain falling – *pitter-patter* – on the ground. Find other words that rhyme in the poem.

◆ Discuss the use of short lines to build up a constant rhythm throughout the poem. Tell the children that they could learn how to clap the beat of the words as they say the poem to make it sound like rain falling. Show them how by clapping the syllables in some of their names. Then begin with the title of the poem. Say and clap the first word. Ask the children to tell you how many claps you made. Repeat for the second word. Then repeat the whole title together. Challenge someone to clap the words of the first line. Discuss the number of claps for each word. Repeat together. Carry on as far as the children are able, saying and clapping the words together.

◆ Tell the children they are now going to find out about syllables in other words to do with school.

◆ Using the differentiated activity sheets

Activity sheet 1

This activity is aimed at children who need further experience of aurally distinguishing syllables in words.

Activity sheet 2

This activity is aimed at children who can sort words by topic and syllable discrimination.

Activity sheet 3

This activity is for children who are more confident in sorting words into syllables and can use a dictionary to find new words.

◆ Plenary session

Bring the whole class together again when the children have completed their tasks. Check the answers for each group by asking children in another group to agree with the given answers. What other words did the children in Groups 2 and 3 find? Do the others agree on the number of syllables for these words? Make a whole class list, in three syllable columns, of all the school words encountered. Challenge the children to add to the lists over the coming week. How many words can they find?

Using poetry
KS1/P1-3

Developing
literacy
Skills

© Hopscotch Educational Publishing

33

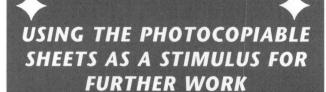

USING THE PHOTOCOPIABLE SHEETS AS A STIMULUS FOR FURTHER WORK

✦ Investigate small words in bigger words by beginning with those on the activity sheets, for example: **jig-saw**, **cup-board**, **paint**ing and tri**angle**.

✦ Make a syllable dictionary of school words with separate topic pages, such as computer words, book words and music words. The pages could be divided into three columns for one-, two- and three-syllable words.

✦ Challenge the children to use the words from the activity sheets as well as words of their own to make up school poems. They could write a two syllable word poem, such as:

> **What is a School?**
> *Pencil, paper,*
> *Apron, ruler,*
> *Jigsaw, table,*
> *Painting, teacher,*
> *Children, playground.*

✦ Make up word searches using school words where the children have to find one-, two- and three-syllable words.

✦ Have a syllable hunt. Provide the children with different coloured stickers for one, two and three syllables. The children could work in groups with a different sticker each. Have a race to place the stickers on objects in the classroom with those numbers of syllables. Which group labelled the most objects correctly?

✦ Play Syllable Snap with pictures of objects of one, two and three syllables.

OTHER IDEAS FOR USING SCHOOL POEMS

✦ Encourage the children to model their own writing on existing poems. For example, ask them to write a number poem about school based on Wes Magee's poem 'Down by the School Gate' (page 60). For example:

> *Ten children write, writing,*
> *Nine teachers talk, talking,*
> *Eight books lean, leaning,*
> *Seven footballs roll, rolling,*
> *Six chairs scrape, scraping,*
> *Five pencils draw, drawing,*
> *Four drums, drum, drumming,*
> *Three brushes, brush, brushing,*
> *Two boys, laugh, laughing,*
> *One hamster, sleep, sleeping.*

✦ Let the children sort through poetry books to find school poems. Ask them to select a favourite and copy it (or a verse) into a class anthology with drawings to match. Ask them to write a sentence saying why they like the poem they have chosen.

✦ Select suitable poems for the children to learn and recite for an assembly about schools.

✦ Use school poems as discussion starters for issues/problems relevant to the children on topics such as bullying and friendships. Use an anthology such as *Please Mrs Butler* by Allan Ahlberg.

✦ Ask the children to select poems that best describe their school. Make a display for the school entrance to welcome visitors to the school.

◆ School words ◆

◆ Look at each picture. Clap and say the word.
  Circle the number of syllables in the word.

1   2   3

1   2   3

1   2   3

1   2   3

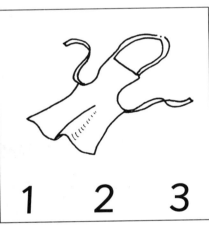

1   2   3

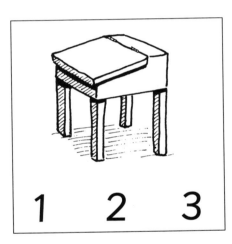

1   2   3

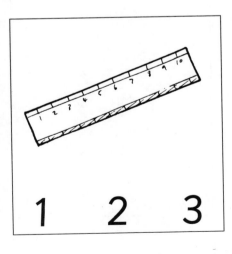

1   2   3

1   2   3

1   2   3

Using poetry
KS1/P1-3

Developing
literacy
Skills

Photocopiable
© Hopscotch Educational Publishing

35

Name _____

◆ School words ◆

✦ Read these words. Circle the things you might find in a school.

book	dog	painting
jigsaw	pencil	desk
tiger	cupboard	bed
computer	bath	telephone
monkey	ruler	chair
triangle	door	scissors

✦ Now sort the school words into the three boxes.

1 syllable	2 syllables	3 syllables

✦ Add one more school word of your own to each box.

Developing
literacy
Skills

Photocopiable

Name _____

◆ School words ◆

◆ These words are in the wrong boxes. Sort them out and write them in the correct box.

1 syllable	2 syllables	3 syllables
caretaker	telephone	painting
apron	book	door
pencil	computer	ruler
triangle	chair	window
jigsaw	desk	table
scissors	corridor	cupboard

1 syllable	2 syllables	3 syllables

◆ Now use a dictionary to help you write some more school words in each box.

Overall aims

- To discuss events and characters in poems.
- To relate poems to own experiences.
- To build a collection of new words relating to a specific culture.
- To use commas to separate items in a list.

 Featured poem (page 61)

Fruits by Valerie Bloom

 **LESSON ONE**

 Intended learning

- To discuss events and characters in a poem.
- To relate poem to own experiences.
- To build a collection of new words relating to a specific culture.

 Starting point: Whole class

- Tell the children that they are going to read a poem from a country called Jamaica. Have they heard of this country? Locate it on a map. Ideally, show them an information book with pictures showing what the country and people look like.
- Explain that the poem is about fruit. Use an enlarged version with the class. Read it one verse at a time. Make sure the chidren can see the words. Before you read each verse, ask them to listen for the name of the fruit mentioned. Write the name of each fruit on the board as you go through the poem.
- At the end of the poem ask the children to tell you what they think was happening. What sort of person is in the poem – is she/he very greedy? How many fruits did he/she eat altogether – count them. What happened to the person at the end of the poem? Why?
- Discuss why the poem uses words that may be unfamiliar to the children such as *mek* (make)

and *you mout* (your mouth). Talk about how that person might speak. Explain that the poet has written the poem to make it sound the way some Jamaican people might speak. Does anyone in the class have a family that originates in Jamaica? Are the children aware that people in different countries and in different parts of Britain speak in different ways?

- Look at the list of fruits written on the board. Circle those the children know. Show pictures of some of the fruits so the children can see what they look like. Discuss what the others might look like. What fruits from the list have the children eaten? Explain that when we buy fruit in a shop it sometimes comes from countries far away. Which fruit on the list do they think can also be grown in this country?

 Group activities

- If possible, obtain as many of the fruits mentioned in the poem as you can. Make labels for each one on card. One group could name and label each fruit with an adult helping. Allow time for them to touch and smell each one and talk about what they look, smell and feel like. Then mix up the labels and ask the children to label them again. Practise saying the names together.
- Some children could write a sentence to describe each fruit.
- More able children could use information books to find out more about the fruit. They could also find out the names of other fruits grown in Jamaica.

 Plenary session

Bring the whole class together again when the children have completed their tasks. Reinforce the names of each fruit by labelling them again and saying the names. Ask some children from each group to share what they found out. What do they think the fruit might taste like? Cut up the fruits and share them out! (Make sure you contact parents first in case of any food allergies.)

38
© Hopscotch Educational Publishing

Developing
Literacy
Skills

Using poetry
KS1/P1–3

◆ LESSON TWO ◆

◆ Intended learning

◆ To use commas to separate items in a list.

◆ Starting point: Whole class

◆ Remind the children about the poem read in Lesson One. Can they remember any of the fruits from the poem? Write up a list and then refer back to the poem to see if they were right. Add any missing fruits to the list.

◆ Tell the children that if they were going shopping to buy the fruits mentioned in the poem, they would need to make a shopping list. By referring to the poem, ask them how much of each fruit they need (half a paw-paw, one guinep, two guava and so on). Write the shopping list using commas to separate each item. Point out the meaning of the commas and why they are used in lists. Tell them about the use of 'and' before the last item on the list. Read out the list together, making sure the children pause at each comma.

◆ Set up a fruit stall in the classroom with real, plastic or pictures of fruit. Try to include as many fruits from the poem 'Fruits' as you can. Make sure all the fruit is labelled. Write some other labels on card with commas on them.

◆ Tell the children that you are going to 'buy' some fruit from the stall by picking up several labels. Set the 'fruit' labels out with 'comma' labels separating each item. Write out the shopping list: 'I went to the fruit shop and I bought...' Ask the children to check that you have put the commas in the right places.

◆ Ask several children to 'buy' some fruit in the same way. Write the sentences on the board, stressing where the capital letters, commas, the word 'and' and the full stop go.

◆ Practise this until you think the children have understood how to use the commas correctly. Tell them they will now have the opportunity to write some sentences of their own using commas.

◆ Using the differentiated activity sheets

Activity sheet 1

This activity is for children who need practice in sorting out the correct sequence of words and punctuation marks before they 'write' the sentence.

Activity sheet 2

This activity requires the children to use all the items in the list provided to write one sentence.

Activity sheet 3

This activity requires the children to make their own decisions about what to 'buy' from a shop. They then write four sentences using commas.

◆ Plenary session

Bring the whole class together again when the children have completed their sentences. Ask someone from each group to read out their work. Does everyone agree where the commas should go? Use the time to reinforce understanding of full stops and capital letters. Ask the children what they would buy if they went to the fruit shop.

Poems from different cultures

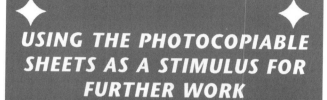

USING THE PHOTOCOPIABLE SHEETS AS A STIMULUS FOR FURTHER WORK

✦ Read recipes from different cultures that use fruits. Cook some of the recipes, then challenge the children to make up their own which also use fruit.

✦ Make a shopping counting book with one long sentence running through it and separate items on each page. Use commas to separate the pages.

✦ Role-play buying fruit at a market. Ask the children to write shopping lists before they 'buy'.

✦ Find out where fruits come from. Find out one word from the language of each country. Teach the children the word and use it during the week.

✦ Read stories that include commas in lists, such as *Don't forget the bacon!* by Pat Hutchins. Use the story to reinforce correct punctuation use.

✦ Make an ABC book of fruits. Write sentences listing the fruits for each letter of the alphabet using commas.

✦ Make up alliterative sentences using fruit names. For example: 'Allan ate an apple, an avocado and an apricot.', 'Penny Patterson picked plenty of pineapples, peaches, pears, paw-paws, plums and pumpkins for Peter.'

✦ Use the lists to make a poem about fruit, for example:
> *Oranges, bananas, apples, pear*
> *Are all on the fruit stall over there.*
> *How many fruits will I buy from you?*
> *Mangoes, paw-paws and guavas too!*

OTHER IDEAS FOR USING POEMS FROM DIFFERENT CULTURES

✦ Make class books on particular cultures, using poems to illustrate way of life, issues, foods, animals and so on. Use the book to make comparisons between the featured culture and the children's own.

✦ Make a display of poems from around the world, showing the location of the poems on a map together with any relevant information books and artefacts.

✦ Ask people from other cultures to share their favourite poems with the class. Use the time to share first-hand knowledge and experiences of the culture.

✦ Ask the children to select a poem that could be used on a travel poster to entice people to visit the country. Look at posters from travel agencies for ideas on presentation.

✦ Write letters to a character in a poem, telling them about the children's own culture/life-style, foods and so on.

✦ Make up a lift-the-flap book with the words 'Where would you find a...'. Select a word from a poem from a different culture. Write this word and draw a picture of it on the flap and then put a copy of the poem inside the flap. Can the children find the word in the poem?

✦ Ask the children to make up a glossary of words to go with a particular poem in order to explain the meaning of unfamiliar words.

Name _____

◆ Fruit ◆

◆ Cut out the words, commas and full stop below to make a shopping list.

I   one orange   one apple

,

.   buy   two mangos

,

will   two bananas   and

◆ Stick your sentence here. Draw a picture of one of the fruits in the list.

◆ Fruit ◆

✦ Look at the names of these fruits.

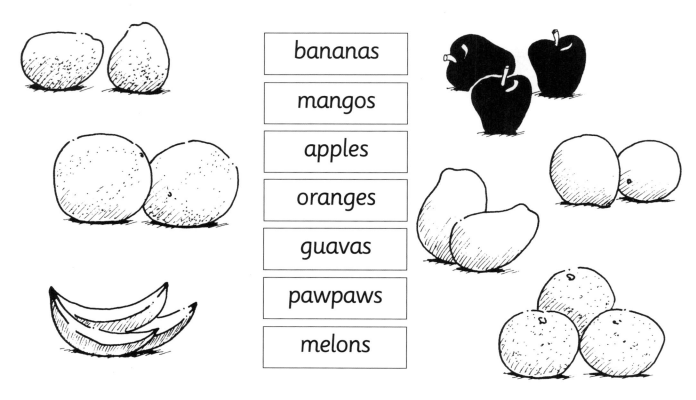

| bananas |
| mangos |
| apples |
| oranges |
| guavas |
| pawpaws |
| melons |

✦ Finish this sentence by using all the names of the fruits above. Remember to use commas in your list.

I went to the shop and I bought some _____

_____

_____

_____

_____

✦ If you were going to buy some fruit, what would you buy? Write a sentence on the back of this page.

Developing
literacy
Skills

◆ Fruit ◆

◆ Decide what you will buy from the fruit shop by completing the sentences. You must buy at least three fruits for each person. Remember to use commas.

 For Mr Mason I will buy _____
_____
_____

 For Michael I will buy _____
_____
_____

 For Janita I will buy _____
_____
_____

 For Sonal I will buy _____
_____
_____

Developing
literacy
Skills

Overall aims

- ✦ To compare poems by the same poet.
- ✦ To identify and discuss favourite poems and poets, using appropriate terms.
- ✦ To use poems as a stimulus for own writing.
- ✦ To write a simple evaluation of a poem, giving reasons.

 ## Featured poems (page 62)

From a Railway Carriage, **My Shadow** and **Autumn Fires** all by Robert Louis Stevenson

 ### LESSON ONE

 ## Intended learning

- ✦ To compare poems by the same poet.
- ✦ To use poems as a stimulus for own writing.

 ## Starting point: Whole class

- ✦ Tell the children that they are going to share some poems all written by the same person, a man called Robert Louis Stevenson. Write his name on the board. Ask them to tell you the special name given to someone who writes poetry (poet). Have any of the children heard of this poet? Do they know any of his poems? If possible, show them an anthology of his poems, such as *A Child's Garden of Verses* (Puffin Classic).
- ✦ Share enlarged versions of Stevenson's poems. You may want to do this over several lessons. What is happening in the poems? Discuss the meaning of each one and any words the children do not understand. Discuss how the reading of a poem can add to its meaning, such as in 'From a Railway Carriage', where the poem can sound like a steam train moving.
- ✦ Compare the different setting out of each poem, using terms such as 'line', 'verse' and 'rhyme'.

 ✦ Ask the children to tell you which poem they like best. Can they say why? Tell them which poem you like best and refer to lines in the poem to illustrate your choice.
- ✦ Ask the children to close their eyes as you read each poem again. As you read, ask the children to picture things in their head. What pictures do they see as you say the words? What kind of train is it? What kind of scenery? How old is the boy with the shadow? What kind of garden is it in 'Autumn Fires'? and so on.
- ✦ Tell the children they will now be able to explore their ideas about the poems further in some group activities.

 ## Group activities

- ✦ Some children could illustrate one of the poems and write relevant captions for the illustrations.
- ✦ Others could write a short description of what they can 'see', imagining that they are the ones on the train, looking at the autumn fires or watching their shadow.
- ✦ One group could select the poem they like best and write down why they like this poem.

✦ Plenary session

Bring the whole class together again when the children have completed their writing tasks. Share the drawings and writing from each group. What captions were used? Are they good ones? Compare the descriptions. Do they sound as if the person is actually there? How effective are the words chosen to describe the scene? What words from the poem were used? How difficult was it to use the poems to imagine words and pictures of our own? Is the poet good at using words and phrases that help us build up images in our minds?

Poet study

 LESSON TWO

Intended learning

♦ To identify and discuss favourite poems and poets, using appropriate terms.

♦ To write a simple evaluation of a poem, giving reasons.

♦ Starting point: Whole class

♦ Remind the children about the work carried out in Lesson One. Tell them that lots of poets, like Stevenson, have written many different kinds of poems and that sometimes these poems turn out to be somebody's favourite. Give them an example of a favourite poem of yours. Tell them why you like the poem so much. Show them the poem in an anthology and read it out to them. Select one line from the poem as your favourite and say why you like this line the best.

♦ Remind the children of some of the poems already known to them – poems they have read this year and/or those in class anthologies. Do they remember some of these poems? Can they remember anything about them? Do any of the children know any of these or other poems off by heart?

♦ Tell the children that they will have an opportunity today to talk and write about their favourite poems. Prepare them for the activity sheets by modelling how to answer the questions, using one of Robert Louis Stevenson's poem as an example. Remind them of the meaning of terms like 'poet', 'poem', 'verse', 'line' and 'rhyme', referring to this poem. Tell them why you personally like the poem. Ask them to help you write your ideas in a sentence. Write the sentence on the board, reminding them about capital letters and full stops. Do the same for a favourite line in the poem.

♦ Give the children time to work in pairs to look through a class poetry anthology before they complete the activity sheets. Encourage them to talk to each other about the poems they read and why they like some of them. You may need to pair up better readers/adults with less able ones.

♦ Using the differentiated activity sheets

Activity sheet 1

This activity provides the children with a very simple framework to make an evaluation of a poem.

Activity sheet 2

This activity requires the children to demonstrate that they understand the content of the poem by illustrating something that happened in the text. It also provides a simple evaluation framework.

Activity sheet 3

This activity is for more able children. It requires them to provide publishing details of the poem as well as information regarding verse, line, rhyme and illustrations (where appropriate).

Plenary session

Bring the whole class together again when the children have completed their evaluations. Ask some children from each group to share their writing. Read out the poems that were selected. Do others also like this poem? Why/why not? Tell the children that although today they were looking at poems they like, it is not necessary to enjoy all the poems they read. Explain that by reading lots of poems they can begin to learn about the things they like and things they do not like about people's writing. Tell them that this also helps them with their own writing. Compare this with reading stories and how we do not all enjoy the same ones.

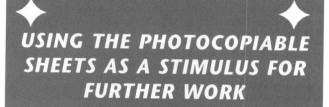

Poet study

USING THE PHOTOCOPIABLE SHEETS AS A STIMULUS FOR FURTHER WORK

✦ Make a class book entitled 'Our Favourite Poems'. Put in copies of the poems mentioned in the activity sheets together with the activity sheets themselves.

✦ Ask the children to learn all or part of their chosen poem to recite to the rest of the class. Use this time to teach how to use the punctuation in the poems correctly and how to recognise when the reading aloud of a poem makes sense and is effective.

✦ Ask the children to work in small groups to dramatise a chosen poem.

✦ Ask the children to write letters to the poet (or publisher) telling them why they like the poem(s) so much.

✦ Make a display of the children's favourite lines from the poems. Use the display to discuss the effective use of adjectives, verbs and nouns.

✦ Encourage the use of indexes by selecting some of the children's favourite poems and making a card to accompany the book from which the poem comes. The card might say: 'Jenny's favourite poem is called... Can you find the page it is on in this book?' or 'Can you find other poems by this poet in this book? Write down the page numbers.'

✦ Ask the children to find out what their parents'/grandparents' favourite poems are. Invite them in to a 'poem sharing' event.

✦ Do a survey to find out the favourite poets/poems of children in the school. Make a display of the results together with the chosen poems.

OTHER IDEAS FOR USING POET STUDIES

✦ Ask the children to make their own anthology books of poems by their favourite poet. They can illustrate the poems and write sentences saying why they like each one. The anthologies could go in the school or class library for others to share.

✦ Invite poets to school to share their poems and the writing process.

✦ Find out information about poets. The Poetry Society, 22 Betterton St, London, WC2H 9BU, will be a good starting point.

✦ Select a poet for the week. Read and share poems by that poet during the week to introduce the children to a wide variety of poetry styles.

✦ Set up a display in the class or school library of the work of one poet. Encourage the children to read the books by selecting interesting/funny/lively poems from the anthologies to whet their appetites.

✦ Compare the poems of different poets on the same theme. How similar/different are the treatments?

✦ My favourite poem ✦

Title of poem: _____

Poet: _____

I like this poem because _____

_____

Copy out your favourite line in the poem here: _____

_____

I like this line best because _____

_____

✦ Draw a picture to go with your poem.

47

✦ My favourite poem ✦

Title of poem: _____

Poet: _____

Why do you like this poem? _____

_____

_____

Copy out your favourite line in the poem here: _____

_____

Why do you like this line best? _____

_____

_____

✦ Draw a picture of something that happens in your poem.
   Label the picture.

◆ My favourite poem ◆

Title of poem: _____

Poet: _____

Title of book: _____

Author/editor: _____

Publisher: _____

What is this poem about? _____

Why do you like it so much? _____

_____

_____

How many verses does the poem have? _____

How many lines in each verse? _____

Write out your favourite line from the poem here: _____

_____

Why is this line your favourite? _____

_____

Does the poem rhyme? _____

If it does, write some words from the poem that rhyme.

_____

Is the poem illustrated? _____

If yes, say what you like or dislike about the illustration.

_____

_____

◆ Read another poem by this poet. On the back of this sheet say
which poem you like best and why.

Overall aims

♦ To discuss meanings of words and phrases that create humour and sound effects in poems.
♦ To use humorous verse as a stimulus for own writing.
♦ To explore words that sound the same but have different meanings.

 ## *Featured poems (page 63)*

A Swamp Romp by Doug Macleod
A collection of tongue-twisters and humorous verse – all anonymous

 ### LESSON ONE

 ## *Intended learning*

♦ To discuss meanings of words and phrases that create humour and sound effects in poems.
♦ To use humorous verse as a stimulus for own writing.

 ## *Starting point: Whole class*

You may choose to use all or some of these suggestions in one lesson or spread the ideas over several lessons.

♦ Ask the children if they like reading funny poems.
♦ Share an enlarged version of 'A peanut sat on the railroad track'. What is funny about this poem? Why does it make us laugh? Do the children know any other funny rhymes like this?
♦ Share an enlarged version of 'Shoeing the Horse'. Discuss the play with words for the past tense. Why has the poet done this? What should the words really be? Explain that poets often play with words to make funny rhymes and phrases. Share 'The Tutor and Tooters' to illustrate this. Explain that such poems are called 'tongue-twisters'. Tell the children they are called this because the words used are very similar to each other, making us stumble with our tongues as we

try to say them. For example: *tutor* and tooter. Discuss how the use of words beginning with 't' makes the sound of tooting as you say the poem. Recite the poem together to emphasise this. Do the children know any other tongue-twisters? Write some on the board and underline the beginning letters of the alliterations. Discuss the use of similar sounding words in these examples.
♦ Tell the children that sometimes poets deliberately use words to make special sound effects. Share 'A Swamp Romp' to illustrate this. Discuss how the words *clomp*, *shiver* and *sludge* can sound like what they mean. Recite the poem again together to emphasise the sounds the words make.

 ## *Group activities*

♦ Some children could write alliterative sentences as tongue-twisters, for example: 'Penny Pepper picked a peppercorn.' In guided writing, an adult could help the children build up the sentences into short tongue-twister verses.
♦ Others could write a list of onomatopoeic words, perhaps on a specific subject, such as the sea or animals. The word list could be used to develop a sound poem similar to 'A Swamp Romp'.
♦ More able children could use the structure of 'Shoeing the Horse' and continue the poem by adding new lines, such as:

I said, "This pencil, sir, will you write?"
And so, the pencil he wrote.
I said, "This cake, sir, will you bite?"
And so, the cake he bote.

 ## *Plenary session*

Share the children's work from each group. Have fun trying to say the tongue-twisters together – who can say them the fastest? Can others think of more words to add to the sentence to make it longer? Share the onomatopoeic word lists. Say the words together. Share ideas about what it is that makes the sentences or poems funny.

◆ LESSON TWO ◆

◆ Intended learning

◆ To discuss meanings of words and phrases that create humour and sound effects in poems.

◆ To explore words that sound the same but have different meanings.

◆ Starting point: Whole class

◆ Ask the children to remind you of the poems and activities shared in Lesson One. Tell them that they are to look at some more funny poems today.

◆ Share an enlarged version of 'Whether or Not'. Ask the children to tell you what is funny about this poem. Discuss the meanings of the words 'whether' and 'weather'. Use a dictionary to help decide definitions. Do they know that there is also another word that sounds the same? Do the children know what a 'wether' is? (male sheep).

◆ Ask them if they know of other words that can sound the same but have different meanings. Write some examples of homophones on the board.

◆ Tell the children that sometimes words can not only sound the same but can also be spelled exactly the same and yet have a different meaning. Give some examples, such as 'match' and 'rule'. Do the children know other words of this kind? Write them on the board and ask the children to use the words in a sentence to demonstrate their meaning.

◆ Share an enlarged version of 'Of All The… ' and ask the children to tell you the two different meanings of the word 'felt'. How does the use of the word make the poem funny?

◆ Finally, share an enlarged version of 'Doctor Bell'. Can the children tell you the word play in the poem? If appropriate, tell them that this kind of word play has a special name – a 'pun'.

◆ Explain to the children that they will now have a chance to explore further those words that sound the same but have different spellings and meanings.

◆ Using the differentiated activity sheets

Activity sheet 1

This activity requires the children to match homophones using visual clues.

Activity sheet 2

This activity requires the children to choose the correct word to complete a sentence so that it makes sense. It encourages them to use a dictionary for support.

Activity sheet 3

This activity requires the children to work more independently, using dictionaries to find out the correct spelling of homophones.

◆ Plenary session

Bring the whole class together again when the children have completed their tasks. Share the meanings of the homophones from each group. Can the children add further homophones for some of these words, for example: rein, rain, reign and buy, by, bye? Do any of the words have several different meanings, for example dear (expensive, term of endearment), herd (a herd of cattle, to herd the cattle)? Challenge the children to think of other homophones not included on the activity sheets. How many can they think of?

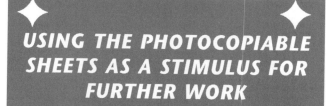

Humorous poems

USING THE PHOTOCOPIABLE SHEETS AS A STIMULUS FOR FURTHER WORK

✦ Ask the children using Activity sheet 1 to write sentences for each word.

✦ Make a class book of homophones, beginning with those on the activity sheets. Ask the children to illustrate the book and use the words in sentences to show their meaning.

✦ Use dictionaries to find out different meanings for the same word. For example: mean = to express something, to intend to do something, to represent something, petty, the middle and so on.

✦ Act out the meanings of words on the activity sheets. Can others guess to which meanings they refer?

✦ Use the words to make up rhymes like 'Of All The…' For example:
  Of all the bees that could ever be,
  This little bee is the best bee to be.

✦ Make up funny verses, using both meanings of the words. For example:
  Mr Care, the big brown <u>bear</u>
  Sunbathed out in the sun.
  But he didn't burn for he wasn't <u>bare</u>
  And so he could have much fun!

✦ Find other poems that use words that sound the same but have different meanings, like 'Doctor Bell'. Make a collection of them.

OTHER IDEAS FOR USING HUMOROUS POEMS

✦ Have fun sharing nonsense poems. A good starting point would be the chapter on nonsense verse in *A World of Poetry*, selected by Michael Rosen (Kingfisher).

✦ Read and share riddles. Make up a class book of riddles.

✦ Invite the children to share jokes. Make a class book of them for all to share.

✦ Invite the children to read simple anthologies, for example: *First Poems*, compiled by Julia Eccleshare (Orchard) or *First Verses*, compiled by John Foster (Oxford University Press) to find poems they find funny. Ask them to say why they think they are funny and get them to classify them into simple types, such as nonsense verse, riddles, tongue-twisters.

✦ Invite the children to select poems for particular purposes, such as 'A poem to make my dad laugh' or 'A poem to cheer up my grumpy teacher!'

✦ Make up funny ABC poems by using alliterative sentences. For example:
  A is for an apple with arms
  B is for a bare bear's bottom
  C is for a caterpillar covered in cream

✦ Share poems that use made-up words, such as 'Jabberwocky' by Lewis Carroll or 'The Loch Ness Monster's Song' by Edwin Morgan. Ask the children to make up their own poems using invented and onomatopoeic words.

◆ Sounds the same ◆

◆ Read these words that sound the same but have different meanings. Draw pictures in the empty boxes.

hare

hair

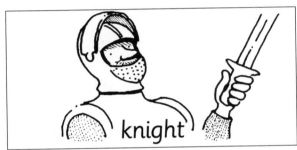
knight

night

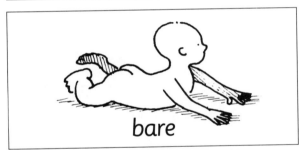
bare

bear

son

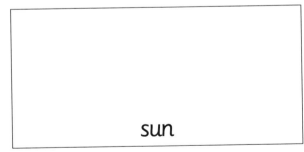
sun

flour

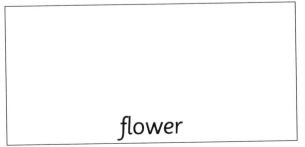
flower

◆ Sounds the same ◆

✦ Complete these sentences by writing the correct word in each space. Use a dictionary to help you.

 Ben went to the shop to _____ some cakes.

| by | buy |

We saw a brown _____ at the zoo.

| bear | bare |

The _____ made some big puddles in the street.

| rein | rain |

The dog's _____ was very wet.

| fir | fur |

 We drove the car along the _____ .

| rode | road |

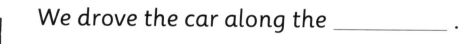 The _____ on the boat was large and white.

| sail | sale |

We are going to _____ a story.

| right | write |

 _____ people do not have any money.

| pour | poor |

The postman delivers our _____ .

| mail | male |

Photocopiable

Name _____

✦ Sounds the same ✦

✦ Write the words that sound the same as those in the chart but are spelled differently. Use a dictionary to help you.

word	sounds the same as
blue	
tail	
break	
heel	
bee	
cheep	
deer	
you	
meet	
herd	
through	
sea	
pail	
caught	
byte	

Developing
Literacy
Skills

Photocopiable
© Hopscotch Educational Publishing

55

Humpty Dumpty

Humpty Dumpty sat on a wall,
Humpty Dumpty had a great fall.
All the king's horses and all the king's men
Couldn't put Humpty together again.

Bat, bat,
Come under my hat,
And I'll give you a slice of bacon;
And when I bake,
I'll give you a cake,
If I'm not mistaken.

Sing, sing,
What shall I sing?
The cat's run away
With the pudding string!
Do, do,
What shall I do?
The cat's run away
With the pudding too!

To market, to market,
To buy a fat pig,
Home again, home again,
Jiggety-jig.

To market, to market,
To buy a fat hog,
Home again, home again,
Jiggety-jog.

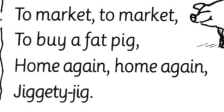

Hickety, pickety, my black hen,
She lays eggs for gentlemen;
Gentlemen come every day
To see what my black hen doth lay.

Developing
literacy
Skills

From: As Wet as a Fish

As wet as a fish – as dry as a bone;
As live as a bird – as dead as a stone;
As plump as a partridge – as poor as a rat;
As strong as a horse – as weak as a cat;
As hard as a flint – as soft as a mole;
As white as a lily – as black as a coal;
As plain as a pike-staff – as rough as a bear;
As tight as a drum – as free as the air.

Anon

One orange owlet
Two tootling trumpets
Three thumping thunders
Four fat farmers
Five funny fools
Six splendid stools
Seven scrumptious stews
Eight elegant emus
Nine neon numbers
Ten terrifying tigers
Are coming your way!

Anon

Hats
A hat for a hamster,
A hat for a dog,
A hat for a goldfish,
A hat for a frog,
A hat for me
To wear in cold weather,
How many hats
Have we got altogether?

Daphne Lister

Pick 'N' Mix Zoo

Marshmallow monkeys,
Crocodile drops,
Red jelly elephants,
Lion lollipops.

Caramel camels,
Butterscotch bears,
Toffee hippopotamus,
Chocolate hares.

Peppermint pandas,
Candy kangaroo,
Strawberry snakes
at the Pick 'N' Mix Zoo.

Celia Warren

Walking Round the Zoo

Walking round the zoo,
What did I see?
An elephant that waved
Its trunk at me.

Walking round the zoo,
What did I see?
A parrot that squawked
And winked at me.

Walking round the zoo,
What did I see?
A crocodile that snapped
Its jaws at me.

Walking round the zoo,
What did I see?
A monkey that pointed
And laughed at me!

John Foster

We can play the Big Bass Drum,
And this is the music to it:
RUM BOOM BOOM goes the Big Bass Drum
And this is the way to do it.

We can play the Bugle Horn,
And this is the music to it:
TA TA TARAH goes the Bugle Horn,
RUM BOOM BOOM goes the Big Bass Drum
And this is the way to do it.

We can play on the Double Bass,
And this is the music to it:
ZOOM ZOOM ZOOM goes the Double Bass,
TA TA TARAH goes the Bugle Horn,
RUM BOOM BOOM goes the Big Bass Drum,
And this is the way to do it.

(Continue:
– TOOTLE TOOTLE TOOT goes the little Flute
– MEENY MINN MINN goes the Violin
– JING A TING TING goes the Tambourine

Anon

The Bird

Here are the legs
that walk along.

Here is the beak
that sings a song.

Here are the wings
that flap and spread.

And here is the bird
above my head.

Tony Mitton

Exercises

Bend your body,
touch your toes.

Straighten up,
and touch your nose.

Wave your arms,
now touch each knee.

Stamp your feet,
and count to three.
One, two, three!

Linda Hammond

58 Using Poetry
KS1/P1–3

Developing
Literacy
Skills

Photocopiable

©Hopscotch Educational Publishing

Granny Granny Please Comb My Hair

Granny Granny please comb my hair
you always take your time
you always take such care

You put me on a cushion
between your knees
you rub a little coconut oil
parting gentle as a breeze

Mummy mummy
she's always in a hurry-hurry rush
she pulls my hair
sometimes she tugs

But Granny
you have all the time
in the world
and when you're finished
you always turn my head and say
"Now who's a nice girl?"

Grace Nichols

Squeezes

We love to squeeze bananas,
We love to squeeze ripe plums.
And when they are feeling sad
We love to squeeze our mums.

Brian Patten

My Dad

My Dad is big and tall,
He has a black beard and no hair at all!
He wears round glasses at a funny angle
And has bushy eyebrows all in a tangle.
He wears the strangest clothes you've ever seen,
To fashionable shops he's never been.
But my Dad's happy, he doesn't mind
What others think of his large behind!
To me, you see, my Dad's the best,
His love for me beats all the rest!

Frances Mackay

Down by the School Gate

There goes the bell
it's half-past three
and down by the school gate
you will see...

...ten mums talk talk talking
nine babies squawk squawking
eight toddlers all squabbling
seven grans on bikes wobbling

six dogs bark bark barking
five cars stopping, parking
four child-minders running
three bus-drivers sunning

two teenagers dating
one lollipop man waiting...

The school is out,
it's half-past three
and the first to the school gate
...is me!

Wes Magee

School is Great

When I'm at home, I just can't wait
To get to school – I think it's great!

Assemblies I could do without,
But I love it, giving hymn-books out.

Writing's fun, when you try each letter,
But sharpening the pencils first – that's better!

Football leaves me with the stitch,
But I'd miss my playtime to mark the pitch.

Cooking cakes gives you a thrill,
But cleaning the bowl out's better still.

Story's nice at the end of the day,
But I'd rather empty the rubbish away.

Yes, school's great – though I'll tell you what:
Going-home-time beats the lot!

Allan Ahlberg

Wet Playtime

hungry chatter
friendly chatter
pitter patter
what's the matter?
tattered textbooks
skim like skates
bad boys batter
last week's mates
watch the rain
just drench the playground
blowing paper
round and round

here inside
the jigsaws clatter
eat those crisps
they'll make you fatter
drop your juice
and dodge the splatter
teacher's coming
quick let's scatter
pitter patter
nitter natter
friendly chatter
what's the matter?

Dave Ward

Developing Literacy Skills

Fruits

Half a paw-paw in the basket
Only one o we can have it,
Wonder which one that will be?
I have a feeling that is me.

One guinep up in the tree
Hanging down there tempting me,
It don't mek no sense to pick it,
One guinep can't feed a cricket.

Two ripe guava pon the shelf,
I know I hide them there meself,
When night come an' it get dark
Me an' them will have a talk.

Three sweet-sop, well I just might
give one o' them a nice big bite,
Cover up the bite jus' so, sis,
Then no one will ever notice.

Four red apple near me chair,
Who so careless put them there?
Them don' know how me love apple?
Well, thank God fe silly people.

Five jew-plum, I can't believe it!
How they know jew-plum's me fav'rit?
But why they hide them in the cupboard?
Cho, people can be so awkward.

Six naseberry, you want a nibble?
Why baby must always dribble?
Come wipe you mout' it don't mek sense
To broadcast the evidence.

Seven mango! What a find,
The smaddy who lef them really kind,
One fe you and six fe me,
If you want more climb the tree.

Eight orange fe Cousin Clem,
but I have just one problem,
How to get rid o' the eight skin
That the orange them come in.

Nine jackfruit! Not even me
can finish nine, but let me see,
I don't suppose that they will miss one
That was hard but now me done.

Ten banana, mek them stay,
I feeling really full today,
Mek me lie down on the bed, quick,
Lawd, a feeling really sick.

Valerie Bloom

From a Railway Carriage

Faster than fairies, faster than witches,
Bridges and houses, hedges and ditches;
And charging along like troops in a battle,
All through the meadows the horses and cattle:
All of the sights of the hill and the plain
Fly as thick as driving rain;
And ever again, in the wink of an eye,
Painted stations whistle by.

Here is a child who clambers and scrambles,
All by himself and gathering brambles;
Here is a tramp who stands and gazes;
And there is the green for stringing the daisies!
Here is a cart run away in the road
Lumping along with man and load;
And here is a mill, and there is a river:
Each a glimpse and gone for ever!

Autumn Fires

In the other gardens
And all up the vale,
From the autumn bonfires
See the smoke trail!
Pleasant summer over
And all the summer flowers,
The red fire blazes,
The grey smoke towers.
Sing a song of seasons!
Something bright in all!
Flowers in the summer,
Fires in the fall!

My Shadow

I have a little shadow that goes in and out with me,
And what can be the use of him is more than I can see.
He is very, very like me from the heels up to the head;
And I see him jump before me, when I jump into my bed.

The funniest thing about him is the way he likes to grow –
Not at all like proper children, which is always very slow;
For he sometimes shoots up taller like an india-rubber ball,
And he sometimes gets so little that there's none of him at all.

He hasn't got a notion of how children ought to play,
And can only make a fool of me in every sort of way.
He stays so close beside me, he's a coward you can see;
I'd think shame to stick to nursie as that shadow sticks to me!

One morning, very early, before the sun was up,
I rose and found the shining dew on every buttercup;
But my lazy little shadow, like an errant sleepy-head,
Had stayed at home behind me and was fast asleep in bed.

Developing
Literacy
Skills

A peanut sat on the railroad track,
His heart was all a–flutter.
Along came a train –
Toot–toot! – peanut butter!

Shoeing the Horse

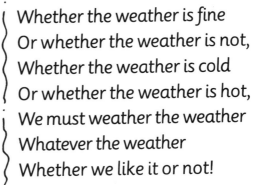

I said, "This horse, sir, will you shoe?"
And so, the horse he shod.
I said, "This deed, sir, will you do?"
And so, the deed, he dod!
I said, "This stick, sir, will you break?"
And so, the stick he broke.
I said, "This coat, sir, will you make?"
And so, the coat, he moke!

Anon

A Swamp Romp

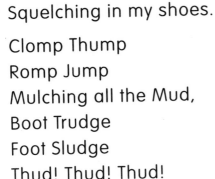

Clomp Thump
Swamp Lump
Plodding in the Ooze,
Belly Shiver
Jelly Quiver
Squelching in my shoes.

Clomp Thump
Romp Jump
Mulching all the Mud,
Boot Trudge
Foot Sludge
Thud! Thud! Thud!

Doug Macleod

Whether or Not

Whether the weather is fine
Or whether the weather is not,
Whether the weather is cold
Or whether the weather is hot,
We must weather the weather
Whatever the weather
Whether we like it or not!

Anon

Of All The…

Of all the felt I ever felt
I never felt a piece of felt
That felt the same as that felt felt,
When I first felt that felt.

Anon

Doctor Bell

Doctor Bell fell down a well
And broke his collar-bone.
Doctors should attend the sick
And leave the well alone.

Anon

The Tutor and Tooters

A tutor who tooted her flute,
Tried to tutor two tooters to toot.
Said the two to the tutor,
"Is it harder to toot or
To tutor two tooters to toot?"

Anon

Name _____